MUSEUM PUZZLE-PICTURE BOOK OF
THE ROMAN ARMY

Sponsored by the Museums Association

Heritage Books & Longman

PREPARING FOR BATTLE

In this picture, a Roman Legion is seen preparing to march out to battle. The soldiers have spent a few days in a temporary camp and some of them can be seen packing up tents and loading them on to carts.

The soldier in the left foreground has put his helmet on back to front to amuse his friends, but the Centurion, who is their officer, looks angry and will soon put an end to their fun.

Spot the differences

In this picture, eight things are missing or have been changed in some way. Look carefully and see if you can spot what they are. You will find the answers on the next two pages.

DID YOU FIND THESE THINGS?

An ear flap is missing from the helmet lying on the ground in the front of the picture. Roman helmets were rather like modern crash helmets – except that they were made of bronze. They were padded inside to absorb the shock of a blow and had neck and ear pieces to give protection from sword cuts.

1

2

The blades of the tools the soldier is loading into the baggage cart are missing. These were trenching tools which Roman soldiers used to dig ditches in order to fortify their camps when they stopped for the night on a long march.

The soldier in the centre of the picture is playing a 'cornu'. The wooden cross-piece by which he held it is missing. It was a musical instrument, rather like a French Horn and was probably used for making trumpet calls in camp and for playing tunes on the march.

3

One of the spokes is missing from the cart in the background. A long column of carts like this followed the Legion on the march. It was called the 'baggage train' and carried spare shields and supplies of many other things needed in battle.

4

The soldier in the left foreground has his sword belt on back to front. These belts were made of leather studded with metal and the apron in front was a form of armour. Belts worns by soldiers had a dagger on the left side; Centurions wore their daggers on the right.

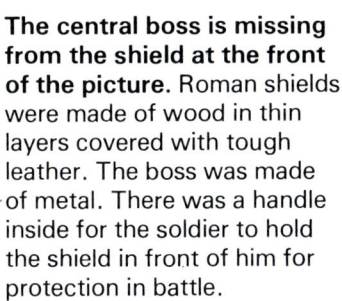

The central boss is missing from the shield at the front of the picture. Roman shields were made of wood in thin layers covered with tough leather. The boss was made of metal. There was a handle inside for the soldier to hold the shield in front of him for protection in battle.

The soldier to the left of the picture wears a sword. The hilt is missing. The hilt is the part of a sword that is held in the hand. Roman swords were about 70 cm long and had sharp points. Ordinary soldiers wore them on their right side; Centurions wore them on the left.

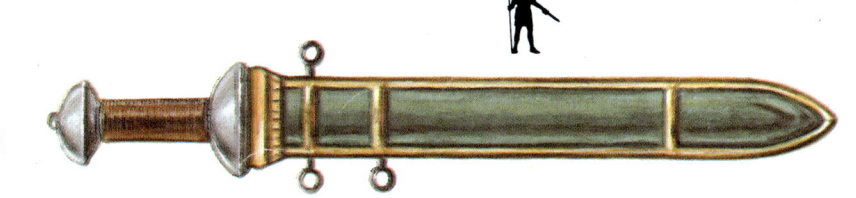

The hand is missing from the top of the standard. Each 'century' – that is, a unit of 80 men with a Centurion in charge – had its own standard. It was a wooden pole decorated with medals, wreaths and ribbons which were awarded for bravery in battle. The soldier carrying the standard was called the 'Signifer' and he wore a bearskin.

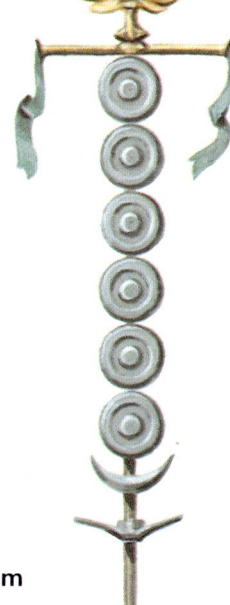

5

MARCHING TO BATTLE

The soldiers of the Legion have now left camp and are marching to war. Archers and lightly armed men have gone ahead to scout for the enemy. In this picture, the Commanders of the Legion have stopped to study the map and decide upon a plan for the battle to come. The soldiers in the column behind are carrying heavy packs and are tired. But they are well trained for war. A Roman soldier had to be able to march 20 Roman miles in 5 hours — 24 miles in an emergency.

Spot the deliberate mistakes

The artist has made eight deliberate mistakes in the picture. See if you can spot them. To find out what they are and why they are wrong, turn to the next two pages.

DID YOU SPOT THESE THINGS?

One of the officers is wearing only one boot. Roman boots were made of leather sewn like modern ones. They had metal studs in the soles to make them last longer. Leather lasts well if it is kept damp and many Roman shoes and boots have been found in swampy land. There are examples in museums.

Half the plume is missing from the helmet of the officer standing third from the right. These plumes, made from feathers or horsehair, could be unclipped from the helmet before battle. Centurions wore their plumes across their helmets; other officers had plumes which fitted on to their helmets from the front to the back.

The horse in the centre of the picture is not wearing a bridle. Roman horses had bridles very much like those we use today. The horses used by the Romans were much smaller than modern ones. It is believed that the ponies that still run wild on Dartmoor, Exmoor and other parts of England and Wales, are descendants of the same horses the Romans found when they came to Britain nearly 2,000 years ago.

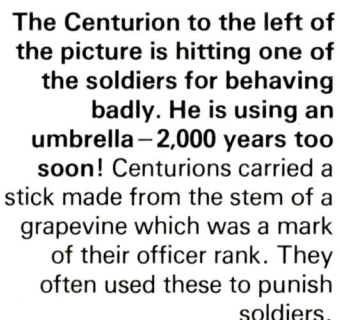

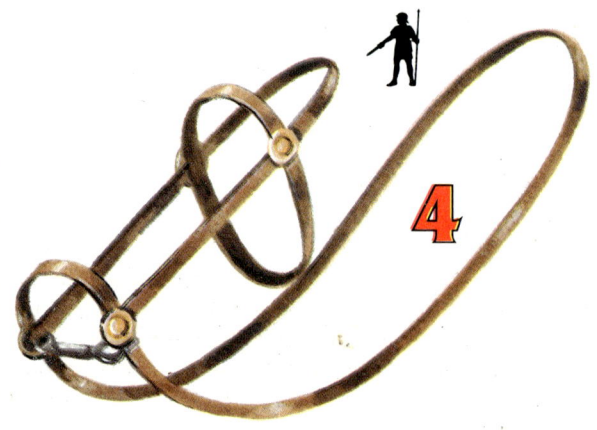

The Centurion to the left of the picture is hitting one of the soldiers for behaving badly. He is using an umbrella – 2,000 years too soon! Centurions carried a stick made from the stem of a grapevine which was a mark of their officer rank. They often used these to punish soldiers.

5 The officer riding the third horse from the right has his feet in stirrups. The Romans did not use stirrups. As can be seen in the picture, their horses were so small that when they were in the saddle, riders' feet were not very far from the ground. The Romans wore spurs like those shown here and these were used to prick the horses to make them go faster.

6 The foot-soldier to the right of the Signifer is wearing the wrong kind of armour. That kind would have been worn by a soldier in England in Tudor times. In the Roman army, soldiers of the Legions wore armour made of overlapping metal plates. These were joined together at the back by strips of leather. The armour was laced up in front.

8 One of the soldiers is carrying a modern transistor radio amongst the baggage on his carrying pole. That is nearly 2,000 years too soon! On the march, Roman soldiers often had to carry very heavy loads. They took with them three days rations of food, a saw, an axe, a trenching tool for digging ditches, a wicker basket for carrying soil, and a mess tin in which they cooked their food. It all weighed nearly 32 lbs (about 23 kilos) – roughly the weight of a large television set.

7 The mounted officer second from the right is not wearing leg armour. This kind of armour was called a 'greave' and was only worn by officers who rode horses. Greaves were made of metal and were usually decorated with elaborate patterns. They were fixed round the calves with leather straps.

9

INTO BATTLE

In this picture the Legion is seen attacking an enemy town. The defenders are lining the city walls, preparing to keep the Romans out. While the Roman heavy artillery pounds the walls with bolts and stones, archers and slingers keep the enemy under constant fire. Under the cover of their missiles, the Roman infantrymen advance to the walls and scale them with ladders. A heavy battering-ram stands ready to knock down the town gates.

Jigsaw puzzle

These jigsaw pieces fit somewhere into the picture and each one contains part of a piece of military equipment that was used by Roman soldiers. See if you can find where each piece fits and say what the things they show were for.
The answers are given in the next two pages.

1 2 3
4 5
6 7 8

DID YOU FIND THESE THINGS?

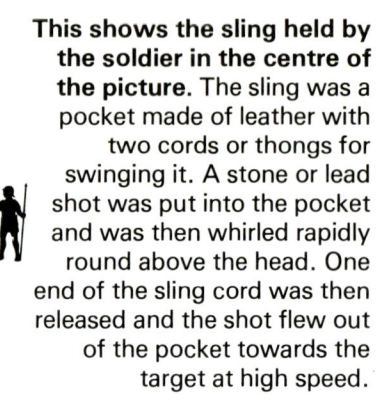

3

This shows the sling held by the soldier in the centre of the picture. The sling was a pocket made of leather with two cords or thongs for swinging it. A stone or lead shot was put into the pocket and was then whirled rapidly round above the head. One end of the sling cord was then released and the shot flew out of the pocket towards the target at high speed.

1

This shows the line of shields sloping toward the city wall. Roman soldiers held their shields above their heads in this special way to protect themselves from enemy missiles. They called the formation a 'Tortoise' because that reptile has a hard shell on its back. Under protection of the Tortoise they could attack heavily defended walls.

2

This shows the javelin being thrown by the soldier in the centre of the picture. The sharp blade of the javelin was only about 4 inches (10 cm) long but it had a long shaft made of soft iron which fitted into a wooden throwing handle.

4

This shows the battering-ram to the right of the picture. This was a heavy beam hung inside a strong wooden frame so that it could be swung backwards and forwards against a door or wall to knock it down. The battering-ram was made from a complete tree trunk which was strengthened at the front end with a metal cap often in the shape of a ram's head.

12

5

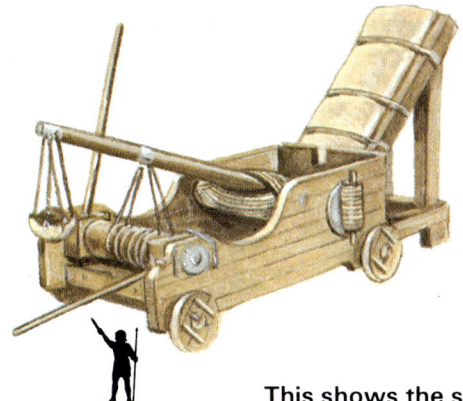

This shows the artillery machine to the left of the picture. This was called an 'onager' or 'wild ass'. It was a mechanical sling able to throw stones weighing as much as 130 lbs (60 kilos) a distance of 220 yds (200 metres). It was called a wild ass because when it was working it made a great noise and 'bucked' like an ass.

This shows the suit of armour worn by one of the archers. It was made up of leather sewn with small overlapping leaves of metal and was lighter to wear than the armour worn by the Roman legionaries.

7

6

This shows the bolt being fired from the other big artillery machine. This was called a 'Ballista' and a drawing of one, showing how it worked, is on page 16. The Romans used these heavy weapons when they were attacking enemy forts, and one fortress they attacked, during the conquest of Britain, was Maiden Castle near Dorchester, in Dorset. The skeleton of one of the Britons found by archaeologists still had a ballista bolt buried in the spine.

This shows the bows the archers are using to fire arrows at the enemy. Archers in the Roman army were foreigners, taken into the army because of their special skill with bows and arrows. Arrow heads have been found at the places where Roman armies fought their battles. Some can be seen in museums.

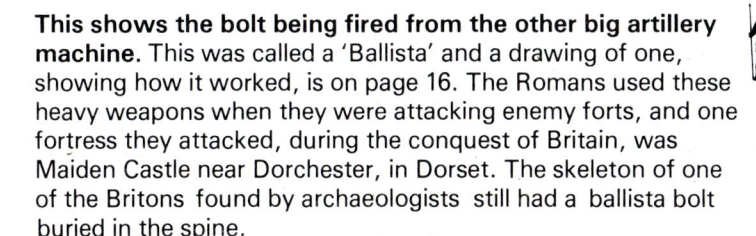

8

13

ABOUT THE ROMAN ARMIES

Why they were famous

The Romans won many famous battles. They conquered many lands to form a great Empire and for nearly a thousand years were the richest and most powerful people in the world. They were able to do this because they had a 'regular' army. Roman soldiers joined up, like modern troops, for an army career. They wore uniforms, marched in step and won medals for bravery. Their battles were fought hand-to-hand and they went into battle on foot or on horseback. They had only oxen or mules to pull their wagons and carts.

Roman armies built their own roads and bridges in order to travel across the countries they conquered. As they had to live in enemy lands, they built high walls round their towns and villages to give protection from attacks. They turned their camps into fortresses when they were on the march, with ditches and fences all round. They conquered every country from Britain to North Africa and from Spain to Egypt.

When their battles were won however, they made friends with their defeated enemies and settled down to live peacefully amongst them. They showed the people they conquered a much better way of life and taught them Roman ways.

How they were trained

It was very important that Roman soldiers should be able to march very long distances at a good, fast pace for that was the only way they could travel on land at that time. The new recruit was trained to march about 13½ miles (21 kilometres) in five hours which is similar to the marching pace of modern armies. The heavy loads they had to carry are described on page 9. They had to be very fit and strong for when they had marched those long distances carrying that heavy load, they sometimes had to go straight into battle. Physical training was important and they practised both high jump and long jump and they all had to learn to swim.

aqueduct

Weapon training

The main weapons used by the Romans were the sword and the javelin. New recruits learned how to use the sword by first practising with heavy wooden staves instead of real swords. Their shields, made of wickerwork, were also far heavier than real ones. They practised against wooden posts, six feet (2 metres) high, pretending that they were enemy troops. They were taught to strike with the point of the sword and not with the edge. When they had become skilled with wooden swords they were given real ones with leather buttons on the points and with these they practised sword fighting, one soldier against another.

The same method of training was used to teach recruits how to throw the javelin. They first used javelins that were much heavier than normal ones and they practised throwing them at the same posts they had attacked with swords.

Fortifying a camp

When Roman armies were on the move, they built a temporary camp at the end of each day's march. If an enemy wanted to attack them the best time would be in the middle of the night when the soldiers, tired after a long march, were fast asleep. To make sure that they were safe from attack, every marching camp was fortified all round, and before they could stop and cook themselves some food, the soldiers had to take out their trenching tools, stack their arms nearby, and start the job of digging a deep ditch. The method was to pile the earth from the ditch to form a high bank and then build a palisade on top of the bank too high for an enemy to climb over. The soldiers usually carried long stakes with them on the march to make into the palisade.

Many sites of Roman marching camps have been found by archaeologists, some of them alongside Roman roads. Many of the things found on these sites can be seen in museums.

a javelin thrower

A ROMAN BALLISTA

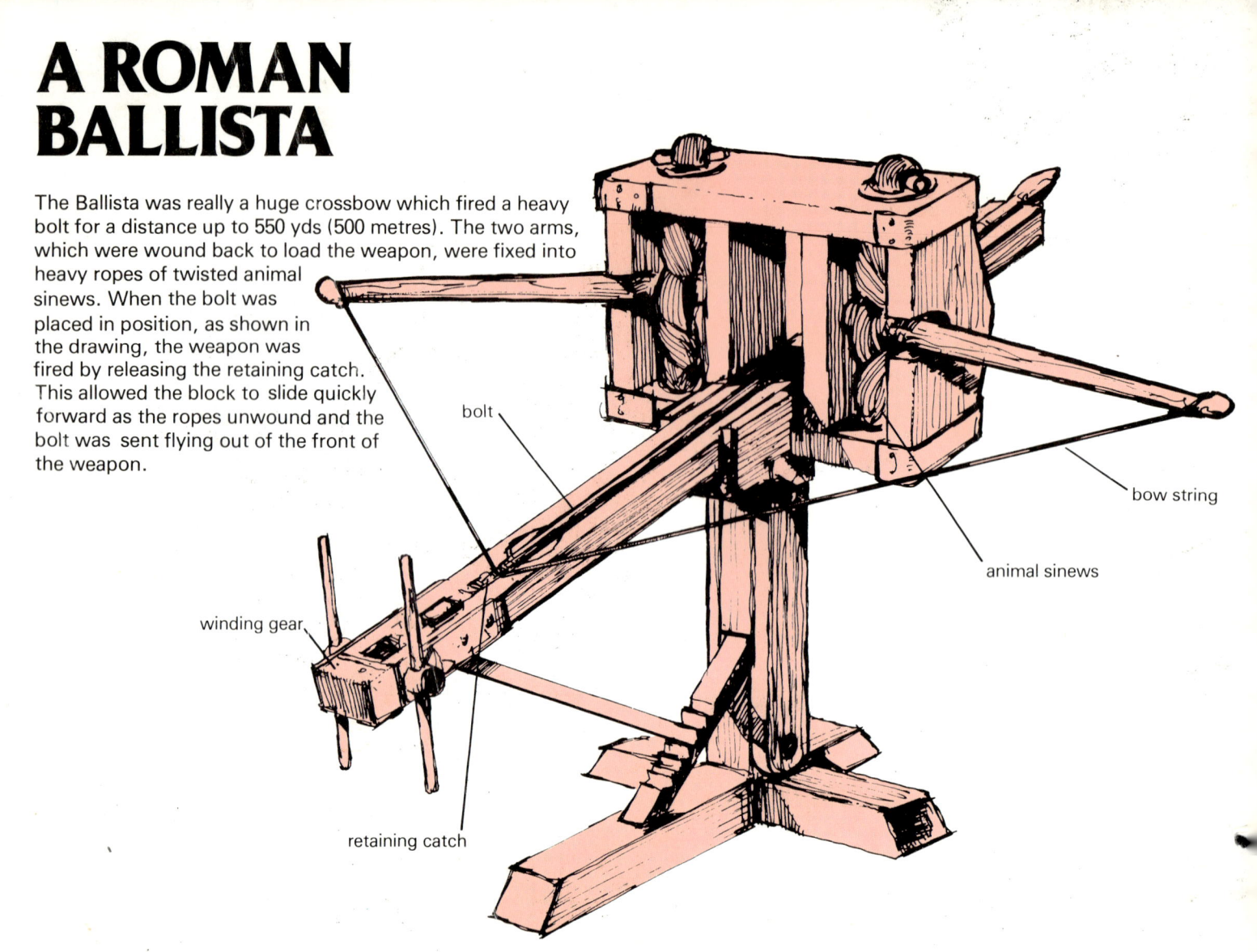

The Ballista was really a huge crossbow which fired a heavy bolt for a distance up to 550 yds (500 metres). The two arms, which were wound back to load the weapon, were fixed into heavy ropes of twisted animal sinews. When the bolt was placed in position, as shown in the drawing, the weapon was fired by releasing the retaining catch. This allowed the block to slide quickly forward as the ropes unwound and the bolt was sent flying out of the front of the weapon.